Gone Forever!
Edmontosaurus

Rupert Matthews

Heinemann Library
Chicago, Illinois

Customer Service 888-454-2279
Visit our website at www.heinemannlibrary.com

Produced for Heinemann Library by White-Thomson Publishing Ltd.
Edited by Kay Barnham
Book design by John Jamieson
Concept design by Ron Kamen and Paul Davies & Associates
Illustrations by James Field (SGA)
Originated by Que-Net Media™
Printed and bound in China by South China Printing Company

08 07 06 05 04
10 9 8 7 6 5 4 3 2 1

Library of Congress Cataloging-in-Publication Data
Matthews, Rupert.
  Edmontosaurus / Rupert Matthews.
    p. cm. -- (Gone forever!)
Summary: Describes what has been learned about the physical features,
behavior, and surroundings of the long-extinct trachodon.
Includes bibliographical references and index.
  ISBN 1-4034-4913-9 (hardcover) -- ISBN 1-4034-4920-1 (pbk.)
  1. Edmontosaurus--Juvenile literature. [1. Edmontosaurus. 2.
Dinosaurs.] I. Title.
  QE862.O65M33 2004
  567.914--dc22
                            2003016685

Acknowledgments
The author and publisher are grateful to the following for permission to reproduce copyright material:
Cover photograph reproduced with permission of GeoScience.
p. 4 Science Photo Library; pp. 6, 14 Camera Press; p. 8 Royal Tyrell Museum/Alberta Community Development; p. 10 Carnegie Museum; pp. 12, 18, 20, 22, 24 American Natural History Museum; pp. 16, 26 GeoScience.

Special thanks to Dr. Peter Makovicky of the Chicago Field Museum for his review of this book.

Some words are shown in bold, **like this.** You can find out what they mean by looking in the glossary.

Contents

Gone Forever!

Many animals that have lived on Earth are now **extinct.** None are left alive anywhere. Scientists called **paleontologists** learn about extinct animals by studying their **fossils,** which are found in rocks.

Edmontosaurus
was a **dinosaur**
that lived millions of
years ago. Other types of dinosaur lived
at the same time as Edmontosaurus.
All of these dinosaurs are now extinct.

Edmontosaurus' Home

Edmontosaurus **fossils,** similar to those above, have been found in rocks in North America. Scientists called **geologists** study these rocks to discover what the land was like when Edmontosaurus was alive.

Edmontosaurus lived on wide, flat land that was close to the sea. There were large rivers and many ponds and lakes. The weather was warm and wet.

Plants and Trees

Edmontosaurus lived in a green world. Much of the land was covered by thick forest. There were **firs, pines,** and **cypresses** such as *Taxodium*. These trees were very tall and kept their leaves all year long.

Taxodium **fossil**

Lots of different plants grew
at the time of Edmontosaurus.
The ground was covered with
ferns. Many bushes were similar
to modern roses, **magnolias,**
and **brambles.**

magnolia

9

Living with Edmontosaurus

Edmontosaurus lived at the same time as many other animals. Saurolophus was a plant-eating **dinosaur,** much like Corythosaurus, which is shown below. Triceratops was another plant-eater. Ornithomimus was a dinosaur that ate small **lizards** and **mammals.**

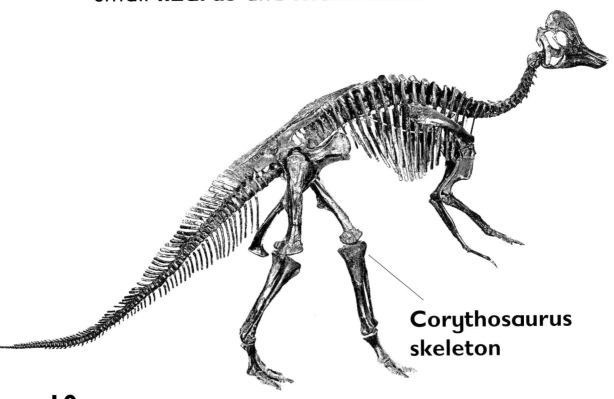

Corythosaurus skeleton

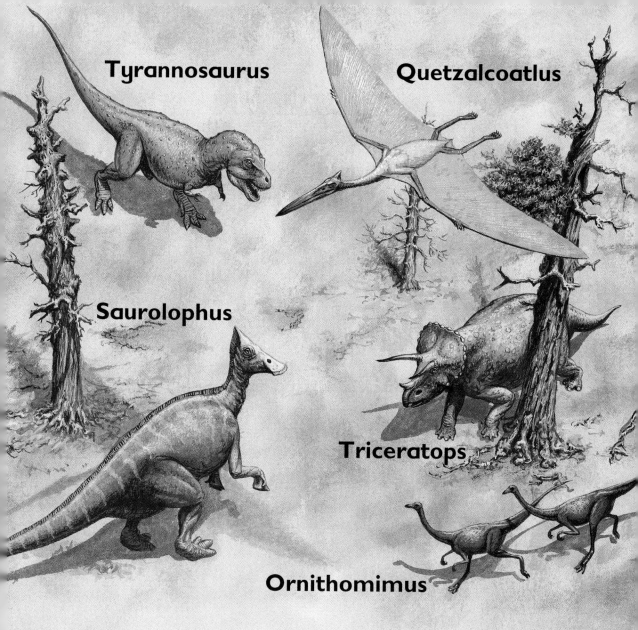

Tyrannosaurus

Quetzalcoatlus

Saurolophus

Triceratops

Ornithomimus

Tyrannosaurus was a **predator** that hunted and ate other dinosaurs. Quetzalcoatlus was a flying **reptile** with enormous wings. All of these animals are now **extinct.**

11

What Was Edmontosaurus?

Scientists study the **fossils** of Edmontosaurus to discover what this animal was like. The bones show how large the **dinosaur** was, how it moved, and how it lived.

Edmontosaurus skeleton

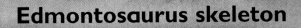

Edmontosaurus was twice as big as an elephant.
It usually walked on all four legs. Each toe had
a strong hoof to support the dinosaur's weight.
Edmontosaurus was a plant-eater.

Baby Edmontosaurus

Scientists have found nests of **dinosaurs** similar to Edmontosaurus. Edmontosaurus probably built the same type of round nest. There was room for about twelve eggs in the nest. The dinosaur may have covered the nest with leaves or mud to keep the eggs safe.

After they **hatched,** the baby dinosaurs stayed in the nest. The adult dinosaurs brought food to their young and may have guarded the nest against meat-eating dinosaurs.

Growing Up

The young Edmontosaurus may have left the nest when they were a few weeks old. At first they may have lived with their brothers and sisters. They would have hidden in the forest to be safe from hunting **dinosaurs.**

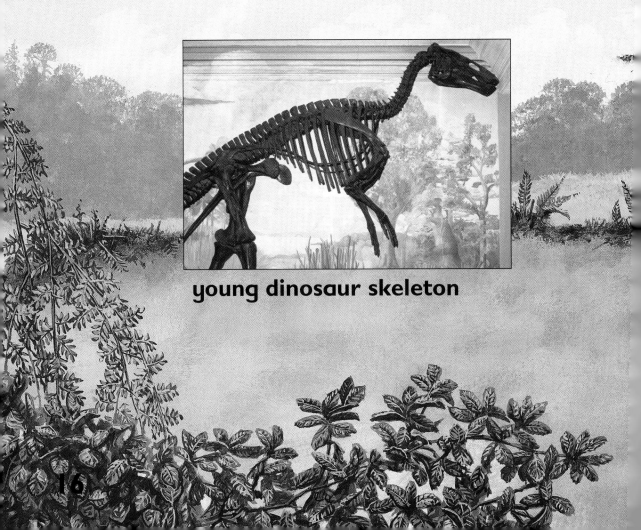

young dinosaur skeleton

As they grew older, the young Edmontosaurus
tried out new types of food. They ate soft, juicy
fruits. When their teeth became stronger, the
young Edmontosaurus ate leaves and twigs.

17

Living Together

Scientists have found **fossil** footprints of **dinosaurs** like Edmontosaurus. The footprints show that the dinosaurs moved in small **herds.** The young Edmontosaurus did not join the adult herd until they were almost fully grown.

A herd was a safe place for Edmontosaurus to live. While some dinosaurs fed, others would keep watch for danger. If a **predator** came near, a few Edmontosaurus might frighten it away.

In the Water

Edmontosaurus' world was very watery, with many rivers and lakes. Edmontosaurus may have spent a lot of time swimming. It could have crossed rivers or **swamps** to find food or eaten plants that grew in the water.

skeleton of Edmontosaurus' tail

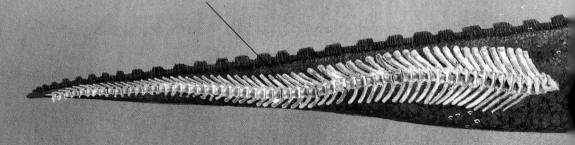

Edmontosaurus may even have swum into deep water to escape from hunting dinosaurs on land. Edmontosaurus was a strong swimmer. It likely swam using its **webbed** feet and powerful leg **muscles.**

Tough to Chew

skull fossil

An adult Edmontosaurus had a sharp **beak.**
At the back of its mouth, there were hundreds
of strong teeth that lay close together. By
studying **fossils,** scientists have worked out
what sort of food Edmontosaurus ate.

Edmontosaurus may have used its beak to bite leaves and twigs off trees and bushes. It could grind the food into a soft paste with its strong teeth before swallowing it. Edmontosaurus ate foods that were too difficult for other **dinosaurs** to chew.

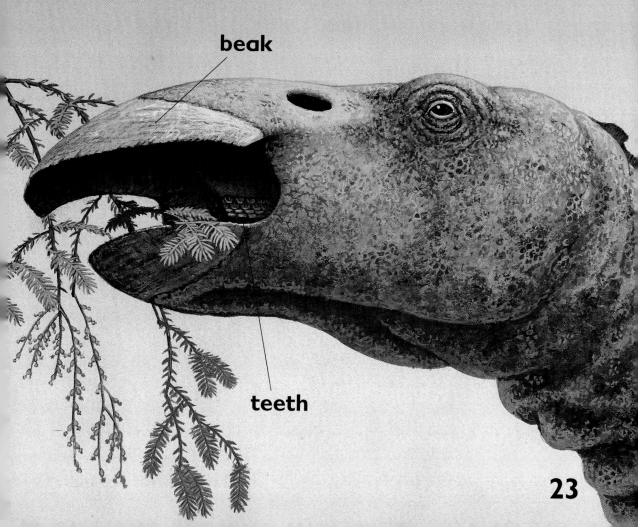

beak

teeth

Run for It!

Edmontosaurus had hooves on all four feet. This shows it spent most of its time walking on all four legs. However, Edmontosaurus' powerful back legs were longer than its front legs. This shows that the **dinosaur** could walk upright, too.

Edmontosaurus would only have been able to move slowly on all fours. It may have stood upright when it wanted to escape from danger. If it used only its back legs, Edmontosaurus could run more quickly.

Dangerous Neighbors

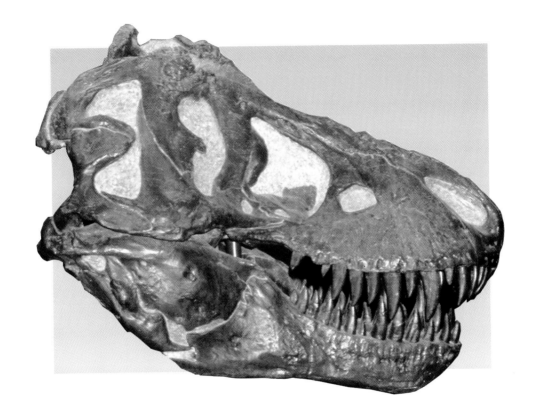

Near the **fossils** of Edmontosaurus, scientists
have found fossils of another **dinosaur.**
These fossils belong to Tyrannosaurus,
a large **predator** with sharp teeth.

Tyrannosaurus may have hunted Edmontosaurus. By hiding among the trees, Tyrannosaurus could have surprised Edmontosaurus and attacked it. However, Edmontosaurus could run to safety if it saw Tyrannosaurus first.

Where Did Edmontosaurus Live?

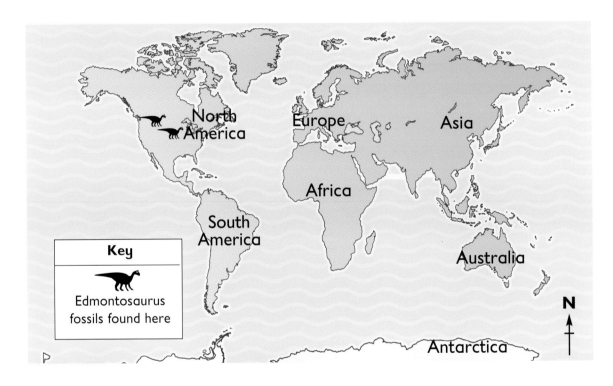

Key

Edmontosaurus fossils found here

North America

Europe

Asia

Africa

South America

Australia

Antarctica

N

Edmontosaurus **fossils** have been found in parts of North America. These show that Edmontosaurus once lived in the areas that are now South Dakota, Wyoming, and Montana in the United States, and Alberta in Canada.

When Did Edmontosaurus Live?

Edmontosaurus lived between 68 and 65 million years ago. This was at the end of the time scientists call the Cretaceous period. The Cretaceous period was the third part of the Mesozoic era, which is also known as the Age of **Dinosaurs.**

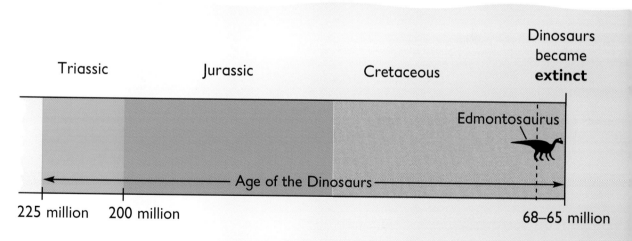

Triassic   Jurassic   Cretaceous   Dinosaurs became **extinct**

Edmontosaurus

← Age of the Dinosaurs →

225 million   200 million   68–65 million

Number of Years Ago

Fact File

Edmontosaurus	
Length:	up to 43 feet (13 meters)
Height:	up to 17 feet (5 meters)
Weight:	up to 3 tons (3 metric tons)
Time:	late Cretaceous period, about 68 to 65 million years ago
Place:	North America

How to Say It

Cretaceous—kreh-tay-shus

dinosaur—dine-o-sawr

Edmontosaurus—ed-mon-to-sawr-us

Jurassic—jer-as-ik

Ornithomimus—or-nith-o-meem-us

Mesozoic—meh-so-zo-ik

paleontologist—pay-lee-on-tah-lo-jist

Quetzalcoatlus—kayt-zal-co-at-lus

Saurolophus—saw-rol-o-fus

Triassic—try-as-ik

Triceratops—try-ser-ah-tops

Tyrannosaurus—ty-ran-o-sawr-us

Glossary

beak   mouth part shaped like the bill of a bird

bramble   prickly plant

cypress   tall tree with leaves that stay green all year

dinosaur   reptile that lived on Earth between 228 and 65 million years ago but has died out

extinct   once lived on Earth but has died out

fern   green plant with large, feathery leaves and no flowers

fossil   remains of a plant or animal, usually found in rocks

fir   tree with flat, needle-shaped leaves that stay green all year

geologist   scientist who studies rocks

herd   group of animals that live together

lizard   small reptile with a long tail

magnolia   tree or bush, usually with creamy-white flowers

mammal   warm-blooded animal with a backbone and hair or fur. Mammals give birth to live young that feed on milk from the mother's body.

muscle   part of an animal's body that makes it move

paleontologist   scientist who studies the fossils of animals or plants that have died out

pine   tree with needle-shaped leaves

predator   animal that hunts and eats other animals

reptile   cold-blooded animal, such as a snake or lizard

swamp   soft, wet land often partly covered with water

webbed   describes feet having toes joined together with skin

More Books to Read

Dahl, Michael. *Dinosaur World*. Minneapolis, Minn.: Picture Window Books, 2003.

Kalman, Bobbie. *What Is a Dinosaur?* New York: Crabtree, 1999.

Scott, Janine. *Discovering Dinosaurs*. Minneapolis, Minn.: Compass Point, 2002.

Index